Charles M. Schulz

I Take My Religion Seriously

WARNER PRESS
Anderson, Indiana

Published by
Warner Press, Inc.
Anderson, Indiana

All scripture passages, unless otherwise indicated, are
from the King James Version ©1972 by Thomas Nelson
or the Revised Standard Version ©1972 by Thomas
Nelson.

Printed in the United States of America
Warner Press, Inc.
Arlo F. Newell, Editor in Chief
Dan Harman, Book Editor

WHY THIS BOOK?

Charles M. Schulz is a warm, comfortable, familiar, and easy-to-love friend of the world. Literally everybody knows him because they have read his mind, his heart, his passions and his foibles in the earth-circling antics of Snoopy and his weird human friends.

You know Charles M. Schulz. He's your pal.

Warner Press publishes this book because you need to know more about "Sparky." He's the kind of person who cares and acts and lives a marvelous life. We won't bore you with the details, but as you look through these cartoon adventures by the artist, take time to thank God for the insights and humorous personal glimpses of the teens, the parents and the pastors that parade through these pages.

"I Take My Religion Seriously" is produced with the full cooperation of Mr. Schulz. Many of the panels reproduced here originally appeared in *Youth* magazine and *Reach.* Some appear here in book form for the first time. As you smile, remember: each panel was personally chosen by Sparky Schulz because it made him smile when he looked at it again.

One of the timeless qualities of these cartoons is that while fashion and terminology may change, the ideas, problems, frustrations, joys, and excitement of teenagers keep repeating, age after age. Why is it that in any city, any church the tallest teen-age boy seems attracted to the shortest girl? Why do youngsters always seem to think that in their deepest frustrations, pastors are supposed to know everything? Everyone knows they don't, but teens keep lashing out with the questions.

Enjoy. There are no hidden messages here. In spite of various attempts to analyze some of the cartoon stars of today's world, these church-related funnies are here just to entertain. You'll see yourself, your pastor, a teacher you knew. You'll get revelations of how your parents felt when you came at them with an earthshaking question. You'll have fun while you shake your head in agreement.

So sit back and enjoy. Pass the book along to a teenage friend.

We did this book to enrich and lighten your life. And Sparky will be happy if you understand that funny things happen all over, far beyond the *Peanuts* setting.

Dan Harman

"You are my dad. I am your son. Isn't that a thrilling thought? How about letting me use the car tonight?"

"We represent the young people of the church, and we've come to you because you're a minister and you know all about everything!"

"Our discussion group misses you, Fred. When you're not there, we don't have anyone to leap on as soon as he opens his mouth!"

"Beat by a girl! It never would have happened, but I hit one of my brilliant streaks of mediocrity!"

"Well, then, let's put it this way. Suppose that, instead of the apple, Eve had offered him a shiny sports car?"

"I just signed up for my fourth straight year at youth camp. I mean—wow—How spiritual can you get?"

"I thought she was saving my letters because she liked me. Now, I found out it's because the church is having a paper drive."

"Standing way up here makes me realize how insignifi-
cant humans are and how stupid you and I are because
now we don't know how to get down again!"

NO,

having our class meet in
the pastor's study is not
the same as being sent to
the Principal's Office.

"I see this is 'Spiritual Life Emphasis Week' in our church. I wonder what it is that we emphasize the rest of the time?"

"Do you think anyone is interested in the number of hot dishes the church has served since the day of Pentecost?"

"Methuselah lived nine hundred and sixty-nine years. That means when he was two hundred years old, he was still a teen-ager!"

"House-to-house visitation, my eye! You stay away from Gloria!"

"Strange thing with Alfred. First we involved him in youth fellowship, then we involved him in men's brotherhood, then we involved him in Sunday school visitation. Finally we involved him right out of the church!"

"Let's face it, sir. What I'm really looking for is a list of good scriptures to memorize in case I get into a violent religious argument and need something to say!"

"Somehow, singing choruses around an electric bar-
becue never seems to do much for me!"

But all I said was,

Understanding you is like trying to understand the Book of Revelation!

"My girl and I have a religious problem, mom. She says *Ah-men* and I say *Ay-men*. Do you think we have a chance to find happiness together?"

"I hope you like them. Who else would think to give you earrings with the Ten Commandments, the Sermon on the Mount, the Twenty-Third Psalm, and pictures of all twelve apostles on them?"

"Oh, no. It looks like we're in for another sermon from the Gospel according to the Reader's Digest."

"What am I supposed to do, eat it or climb it?"

"I'm very happy to be part of a confused generation because I never have been able to figure out whether I'm coming or going!"

"I'm glad you brought that verse up for discussion because I just happen to have a set of Bible Commentaries with me!"

"So how do I know why he ate locusts? Maybe there weren't any drive-ins around!"

"I used to consider myself an authority on the Book of Revelation, but one day I came across somebody who had read it."

"I've been wanting to ask you something, Reverend Palmquist. At what age did you decide to become straitlaced?"

"Instead of bringing you a corsage, I think you'll be glad to know I have donated a gift to the youth fellowship in your name!"

"Then again, what happens if the world comes to an end before I grow up, and get a chance to become a minister and warn everybody about the world coming to an end?"

"I may not work very fast, but I sure do a sloppy job!"

"Other people put a shell to their ear and hear the ocean roar. He hears Handel's 'Hallelujah Chorus!' "

"I realize that we all have to do our part in these youth fellowship parties, but there's something humiliating about being put in charge of bringing the toothpicks!"

"Here's the church and here's the steeple. Open the door, and see how few people turned out for Wednesday night prayer meeting!"

"I think the presence of my car does a lot for our church. It proves we're a struggling young congregation!"

OF COURSE,

I brought something for the picnic... I brought the most important thing I could think of...

ME!

"I think I like pledging better than tithing. It doesn't involve so much arithmetic!"

"I hope my investing in a new set of tires doesn't give you the impression that I don't believe your preaching about the world coming to an end, Rev. Meyers."

"How can you be a good Christian when your stomach hurts?"

"She's my cousin from Minneapolis. Tell Harold I think he'll like her. She's a real football fan!"

"Next Sunday evening we are going to have a combined
meeting with the youth fellowship of the church across
the street to find out which separates us the most—
'doctrine or a street full of traffic.'"

"You've given me one of your tracts, sir, and I've given you one of mine. Now, where do we stand?"

"And this is my Uncle Joel on my mother's side. They say he's very religious. He's against all forms of entertainment except pitching horse shoes!"

"So how can I kneel in front of my bed to say my prayers? I sleep in the upper bunk!"

"And then I thought I'd conclude with an illustration of how important it is not to hide your light under a bushel!"

DON'T BOTHER ME...

I'm looking for a verse of scripture to back up one of my preconceived notions!

"I can understand your wanting to be a medical missionary, but how can you love the whole world so much, and still not like ME enough to go roller skating next Friday?"

"This is the most modern translation of the Bible ever published. Instead of the word God, they use the term 'The Man Upstairs!' "

"Pardon me, but I've never talked with a nun before. Do you speak English or Latin?"

"The insane suggestion that we purchase twelve-hundred dollar stereo systems for each of the Sunday school rooms has been turned down. Is there any more old business?"

"I've been feeling kind of depressed, Reverend Penning-
ton. I think what I need is a spiritual Band-Aid!"

"I just read where all girls eventually end up resembling their mothers, so before I ask you for a date, I was wondering if you happened to have a snapshot of your mother with you?"

"Congratulations, mom. You're the only mother I know who has a son who has studied his Sunday school lessons for seven years in advance!"

You're my kind of girl...

YOU'RE A GIRL!

"Haven't you heard? Right after the evening service
there's going to be a wiener roast!"

"I'm in charge of devotions at youth fellowship tomor-
row night, dad. Tell me all there is to know about the
Bible!"

"These are perfect attendance pins—Sunday school, youth fellowship, youth leader training, men's brotherhood, youth work night, men's work night, youth missions, youth recreation, vacation school, Bible camp, youth Bible camp, city youth camp, county youth camp, state youth camp, international youth camp, and choir practice—I haven't been home in three months!"

"Six dollars and forty-five cents? Wow! I had no idea I was paying for the feast of Belshazzar!"

"The Gideons put a Bible in every hotel room, don't they, sir? Well, my idea is to put a Bible in every glove compartment!"

"I wish ol' King Herod had been here, Brother Forbes.
You would have had him all shook up!"

"If we won't have mothers and fathers up in heaven, mom, what do you think you'd like to have me call you?"

"This is church clean-up day—I've mowed the lawn, scrubbed the front steps, and raked all the leaves. Now I'm cleaning the minister's glasses!"

"I'm not interested in becoming real educated, dad. I just want to be like the average adult, and feel that I know all the answers!"

We disagree theologically...

HE THINKS
HE'S
PERFECT,

AND I
THINK HE
ISN'T!

"Oh, yeah? Well, I'll bet my Bible has more passages underlined than your Bible!"

" 'In the beginning God created the Heaven and the Earth!' How's that for being able to quote the scripture?"

"I wonder if there's such a thing as a spiritual dentist? I think my whole personality is full of cavities!"

"All right. A motion has been made and seconded that even though Fred, here, interprets the story of Jonah and the fish allegorically, he can still be permitted to attend our youth fellowship picnic."

"So she's a little tall. Be proud of her. It's not every guy who can date a girl who played Goliath in a Sunday school pageant!"

"I like you because you like me, but that's not a very good reason for liking someone, so I think we should stop seeing each other!"

"Did you ever have a dream that really shook you up, mom? Last night I dreamed that Albert Schweitzer was beating me over the head with a Sunday school quarterly!"

"Psst. You've prayed for the poor people, the rich people, the church, the heathen, our country, and the weather—leave ME something to pray for!"

"OVERDUE? How could this book be overdue when I've only read the first two chapters?"

"I'm sorry, I should have warned you—never hold our family Bible upside down!"

"I enjoyed your sermon on young people, Reverend Morgan. I almost got the impression that you were human once yourself!"

"I wasn't trying to be insulting. All I said was that I had read the entire book of Jeremiah while I've been waiting for you!"

" 'In the early days, Christians who were persecuted
sometimes hid in the catechisms.' No, I don't think
that's quite right."

"I have to hang up now, Gloria. My dad is ready to give me another driving lesson!"

"According to the thirtieth verse in the tenth chapter of Matthew, 'the very hairs of your head are all numbered.' When are you going to take those hairs down to the barber shop and get them cut?"

". . . and then after that we'll go to some fancy restaurant for supper, unless, of course, you'd rather we'd just spend the whole evening at your house—hint, hint, hint!"

...and he will be speaking to us on the SUBJECT,

"Did Joshua really make the SUN STAND STILL?"

"I think she's the most beautiful girl I've seen in my whole life—or rather, this year—this month—this week—well, maybe during the last twenty minutes."

"Choir practice ended early tonight, dad. The pianist and the choir leader got into an argument during the singing of 'Love Divine!'"

"Could you hold the line for just a moment? I think I'm about to be hit on the head with my own shoe!"

"What do you mean, I'm not as spiritual as I could be? I bowl in *three* church leagues, don't I?!"

"See that new church? I helped fix the flat tire on the truck that hauled the papers for the paper sale that paid for the wood that they used to build the front steps!"

"I'll never be a good song leader. Trying to decide whether we should sing the first, second, and fourth verses, or the first, third, and fourth verses or the first, fourth, and fifth verses is driving me crazy!"

"I think maybe I've discovered my trouble with getting out of bed, mom. I think I'm allergic to morning!"

"The Bible contains 3,566,480 letters and 773,893 words. How's that for a bit of useless theological information?"

"Let's be good sports, and play a fair game. Our team promises not to pray for a victory if your team will promise not to pray for a victory."

"You can relax. There's not a thing in the entire book of Leviticus against wearing contact lenses!"

"If you really like me, you'd come and watch me play softball, but I'm glad you're not, because I don't want you to see what a terrible player I am!"

"I was real glad to hear that you're the new chairman of the church's Board of Trustees, dad. I've always wanted a friend among the hierarchy!"

"It started out to be a great painting of Shadrach, Meshach, and Abednego, but everyone tells me it looks more like the Three Stooges!"

"Someday when I get to be rich and famous, I wonder if I'll still be the same sweet, lovable, humble person I am now."

"Sure, I can listen to the radio, watch TV, read a book, and talk on the telephone all at the same time, but I will admit that I'm glad breathing is automatic!"

"I wonder what Luke would have recommended for the relief of the pain of headache?"

I'm sorry, but I wasn't able to study the lesson
FOR THIS
SUNDAY...

The zipper on my Bible is stuck!

"I think I'd like to devote my life to working with underprivileged young people, dad. You know, with guys who are forced to own cars that are at least five years old."

"Do you want to meet me after school but before Hi-Y, or after Hi-Y but before student council, or after student council but before youth fellowship?"

"I have been told that to make a boy like you, you have to learn to talk about the subject he is most interested in. Do you have any books on eating?"

"This radio preacher is really wound up tonight!"

"I nominate Fred for program chairman because he's a young man with ideas and lots of drive and because we all know that nobody else will take the job!"

"Here comes Harold. The first time he says, 'Let's greet the brethren with a holy kiss,' he gets slugged!"

"Mom, I've decided to try to be perfect. Will you mind having someone hanging around the house who is perfect?"

MY
BIBLE
IS HOLIER THAN YOUR
BIBLE.

It has thinner pages!

"I appreciate being nominated as president of our youth group, but I am afraid that I must decline on the grounds that I am too stupid!"

"For weeks we've been planning this youth fellowship picnic, and now we have to call it off because of rain. What I want to know is, who sinned?!"

"I find the gospel very easy to understand. What confuses me is theology!"

"I've decided to go on to college, dad, and then, after that, try to become a 'Prophet of Doom!' "

"How come Shakespeare, Rembrandt, and Beethoven never belonged to our denomination?"

"I like you, Mildred, because you're the kind of a girl a
guy can talk to. Mildred? Mildred?"

"I had to give up having a secret closet of prayer. Every time I went in there, all those cashmere sweaters made me feel guilty!"

"Perhaps I lack real spiritual dedication, but there are certain things about visitation work that drive me crazy!"

"I just thought I'd introduce myself because I noticed your offering envelope was next to my offering envelope in the collection plate."

"Do you think Dial-a-Prayer will be offended? I accidentally hung up without saying amen!"

"He always prays for greater understanding like he's afraid he might get it!"

"Another good thing about just sitting looking into a
fire is there aren't any commercials!"

" 'The minutes of the last meeting were read and accepted.' Isn't that wonderful? That sort of gets me right here!"

"Wally Nelson will now lead us in a discussion entitled, 'It doesn't matter what you believe, just so you believe something!'"

"Sure, I know all about that beautiful coat that Jacob gave Joseph, but I'll bet you that Joseph didn't already have seven sport coats at home!"

"Jacob worked for Rachel's family for seven years to obtain her hand in marriage. I can't even find a boy friend who will help my mother carry the groceries in from the station wagon!"

"I'll bet the churches at Ephesus, Smyrna, Pergamum, Thyatira, Sardis, Philadelphia, and Laodicea never ever heard of crab grass!"

"Either we're going to have a special number on the musical saw, or I'm sitting next to a member of the building committee."

"My finances are in sad shape, Gloria. I've not only robbed Peter to pay Paul, I've also robbed Matthew, Mark, Luke, and John!"

"The Hymnal"

First Verse   Second Verse   Third Verse   Fourth Verse

"Scholars have been disputing this passage of scripture for years, but this morning I'm going to give you the real scoop!"

"Why aren't you in Sunday school?"

"I can't seem to get a strike to save my soul, but fortunately, the salvation of my soul doesn't depend upon my getting a strike!"

"Do you ever look up at the stars and wonder what's beyond the space out there beyond what is out there beyond whatever is out there?"